For Shelley, with thanks for the inspiration – J.M.

*For Nathalie, Francesca and Carmen Rodriguez
and Toby and Zac Uberoi – C.B.*

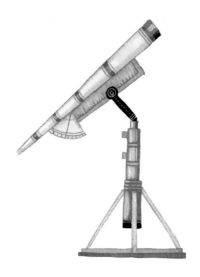

First published in Great Britain in 2004 by
Frances Lincoln Children's Books, 4 Torriano Mews,
Torriano Avenue, London NW5 2RZ
www.franceslincoln.com

Distributed in the USA by Publishers Group West

British Library Cataloguing in Publication Data available on request

ISBN 1-84507-074-7

Set in Frutiger and Minion

Printed in China
3 5 7 9 8 6 4 2

ZODIAC

Celestial Circle of the Sun

Jacqueline Mitton
Illustrated by Christina Balit

FRANCES LINCOLN

Introducing the Zodiac

Twelve of the most well-known constellations belong to the Zodiac, circling the heavens like a belt. If we could see the stars by day, we would observe the Sun slowly making a journey around the Zodiac once a year. The Moon and planets also keep within the Zodiac band, or close to it, as they move against the background of distant stars.

The Zodiac is a strange collection of human figures, real and mythical creatures, and just one non-living thing – the Scales. These curious symbols have been handed down to us through a long tradition, beginning with the sky-watchers of ancient Mesopotamia. Some of the Zodiac constellations we use today were recorded on clay tablets dating from around 1100 BC and the origins of a few – the Bull, the Lion and the Scorpion – go back even further, to around 3000 BC.

By 500 BC, Babylonian astronomers had divided the band of the Zodiac into 12 equal sections or 'signs', and were recording how the Sun,

Moon and planets moved through the signs. At about the same time, astrologers started casting horoscopes based on the positions of the Sun, Moon and planets in the Zodiac. Greek astronomers of the time adopted the Zodiac, and Greek poets and writers linked some of the Zodiac constellations with their mythology.

Astrologers still follow the system of equal Zodiac signs invented in Mesopotamia over 2000 years ago. Today's astronomers continue to use the ancient Zodiac constellations, though they are now precisely defined with straight-line borders around different-sized areas of sky. The names of the Zodiac signs and constellations, and the figures associated with them, are familiar to millions of people all over the world. We owe it all to the creative imagination of the ancient civilisations of the Middle East.

ARIES

How serenely Aries the Ram sits, admiring his magnificent fleece! A trio of stars marks his head, chief among them a yellow giant called Hamal. Though not a prominent constellation, Aries is considered the first of the Zodiac signs and this is the reason why. In March, the Sun crosses the celestial equator from south to north. On this day, known as the equinox, daytime and night are each twelve hours long. Between two and four thousand years ago, the Sun happened to be in Aries at this significant moment. So the Ram was seen as the leader of the flocks of stars circling around the sky.

In ancient Greek mythology, Aries became the magical flying Ram with the golden fleece. The legend tells how Zeus sent a ram to rescue Phrixus, son of the King of Boeotia. The unfortunate youth was about to be sacrificed, victim of a plot by his jealous stepmother. But Zeus' ram whisked him off, along with his sister Helle, and soared up into the air. Losing her grip, poor Helle fell to her death. But Phrixus held on tight until he landed safely in Colchis. In gratitude, he sacrificed the ram to Zeus. Its golden fleece was hung in the temple of Ares and its lasting memorial shines up in the stars.

TAURUS

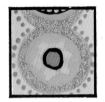 Four thousand years ago, Mesopotamian sky-watchers saw the face of the Bull of Heaven where the Hyades star-cluster shines like silver freckles on his nose. His long horns are tipped by white, jewel-like stars, and the vivid orange star Aldebaran sets his eye aflame.

The stars clustering on the Bull's neck are the Pleiades, sisters who numbered seven, according to tradition. Most people can see no more than six with the naked eye, though astronomers have counted hundreds with the help of telescopes. According to Greek myth, the Pleiades and Hyades were daughters of the giant Atlas, set in the sky by Zeus.

Taurus has always been a potent symbol of virility and steadfastness. Some people believed him to be a mighty god in disguise – Osiris or Zeus. And for some he was the bull sent by the ocean god Poseidon when Minos, ruler of Crete, prayed to him. Minos promised to sacrifice the bull if Poseidon answered his plea for a sign from the gods. But when the cheating king failed to keep his side of the bargain, Poseidon took revenge by cursing Minos' wife with a passion for the bull. Her offspring, the monstrous Minotaur, was born with a bull's head on the body of a man.

An even older Babylonian tale says that the sky god Anu created the celestial Bull at the request of his daughter Ishtar, the warrior goddess of love.

GEMINI

Inseparably intertwined, the Twins gaze down on us from the sky. Two of the Zodiac's brightest stars shining at their heads have been called 'the Celestial Twins' ever since ancient times. But although they are closely matched in brilliance, by nature the Twins are not alike. Pollux, the brighter, more southerly star, is an orange giant. His brother, Castor, looking steely-white, is a rare phenomenon of space – not one star but six, tied together in a close-knit group by the binding power of gravity.

Each year on 13th or 14th December, a rain of falling stars pours from Gemini, like sparks from a firework in the sky. For all their dazzle, these fleeting lights are no more than specks of dust, shed long ago into space from a comet's tail, now burning up when they plunge into Earth's atmosphere.

Castor and Pollux were mythical heroes of Sparta. Though they were born together, Pollux was the immortal son of Zeus and Castor the mortal son of King Tyndareus. When Castor was slain, grief-stricken Pollux refused to be immortal unless his brother could be immortal too. Zeus was moved by their devotion to each other. He set the Twins' image in the heavens and allowed them to stay together, alternating their days between the realm of the gods and Hades, home of the dead.

CANCER

 Of all the constellations in the Zodiac, the Crab is the faintest. With its feeble stars, it is as indistinct as a seaside crab half-buried in the sandy shore.

On one day in June, the Sun reaches the most northerly point of its annual journey around the sky. Two or three thousand years ago, the Sun was in Cancer when it arrived at this solstice, the turning-point in its path. Mesopotamian people said that it marked the gate through which human souls passed on their way from the heavens to the world below. The Egyptians identified the stars at this auspicious celestial place, not with a Crab, but with their sacred scarab beetle, a symbol of fertility, life and rebirth.

The ancient Greeks said that Cancer was the crab that bit the foot of the hero Heracles as he strove to kill the Hydra, a many-headed monster. The crab took sides with Hera, the wrathful jealous goddess who hated the hero. Heracles crushed the crab under his heel in a trice. Afterwards, Hera placed it in the stars.

But the Greeks also told another story about some of Cancer's stars. A hazy, Moon-sized cluster of 200 stars, known as 'the Manger', rides on the back of his shell. The two stars on either side of the Manger were named to commemorate a famous pair of donkeys. Ridden by the Olympian gods in their battle against the Titans, the plucky asses brayed so loudly that they scared the attacking giants away. It is said the donkeys were put in the heavens by one of their riders, Dionysus.

LEO

 Since time immemorial, sky-watchers everywhere have discerned the shape of a lion in the stars, and have hailed the King of the Beasts as a regal constellation. An arc of stars outlines his head, curving around in the shape of a sickle. On his shaggy mane Algieba shines, a close pair of golden-yellow stellar giants. Leo's brightest star burns white-hot close to his heart. Named Regulus, it was the foremost of the ancient Royal Stars of Persia.

As an emblem of strength, Leo has been linked throughout history with the power of the life-giving Sun. He was sacred to the Egyptians because he heralded the return of the waters of the River Nile. As the Sun entered Leo, the season began when the flooding of the river made barren ground fertile once more.

Looking for a myth to explain the celestial Lion, the ancient Greeks turned to the tales of Heracles and the first of the twelve labours he performed. The land of Nemea was ravaged by an invulnerable lion. Neither fire nor metal could penetrate its skin. Somehow Heracles had to kill the fearsome beast. First he cornered the lion in the cave it used as a den, then he strangled it, using only his bare hands. He flayed the lion's skin with the creature's own claw and wore it ever after as armour.

VIRGO

 Dazzling white Spica, Virgo's brightest star, marks a ripe ear of corn in the maiden's hand. Less brilliant stars softly outline the female figure drifting the length of the Zodiac. She is the largest but one of all the constellations.

Many different stories have been told about her. In ancient Greece, some said Virgo represented Justice and was Zeus' daughter Dike. She lived with mortals in a Golden Age long ago, when peace and order reigned on Earth. But when wars and conflicts began, and humans stopped upholding the law, she fled up to the heavens. Others said she was Erigone, daughter of King Icarius. A gift of wine from Dionysus brought misfortune on them both, for when Icarius was murdered by drunken shepherds, Erigone was so overwhelmed by grief, she killed herself. Afterwards Erigone, her father and their dog all became constellations.

But above all, according to the most ancient tradition, first Spica, then Virgo have stood as symbols for corn, the harvest and fertility. Demeter, Earth goddess of the ancient Greeks, is another of her identities. As the loving mother of Persephone, Demeter pines all winter long because her daughter must live in the Underworld with her husband Hades. Seeds lie dormant in the ground until Persephone reappears with the first green shoots in spring.

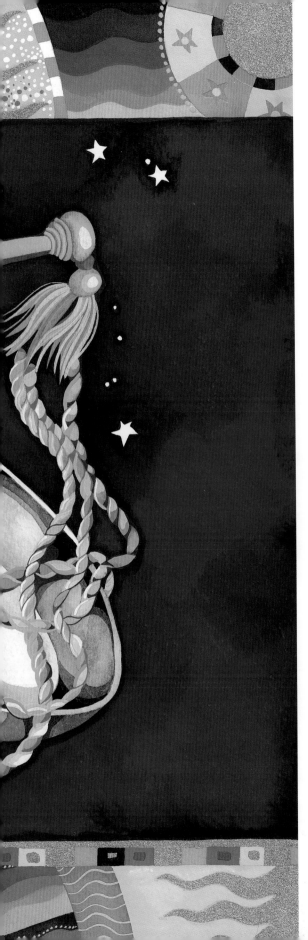

LIBRA

 If Virgo is Justice, then Libra could be her scales; its faint stars hang lightly below her feet. Libra fills a one-twelfth section of the Zodiac where there is no striking pattern among the dim, scattered stars.

The ancient Greeks did not see scales here. Instead, they perceived a pair of claws, stretching out in the sky from neighbouring Scorpius, even though a thousand years earlier these same stars were known as 'the Scales of Heaven' in Mesopotamia. At that time, some two or three thousand years ago, the Sun was in Libra at one of the two equinoxes of the year – the pivotal moment in September when the number of hours of night and daylight are evenly balanced at twelve.

The Romans settled the disputed constellation name in the time of Julius Caesar. They bequeathed to us the name 'Libra', a tribute to the Emperor who declared he was the fount of justice for his people. But the Greek tradition has left its legacy too: the Arabic names for Libra's two brightest stars – Zubenelgenubi and Zubeneschamali – mean 'the Northern Claw' and 'the Southern Claw'.

SCORPIUS

Dazzling Scorpius is like a jewel set with precious stones and pinned to the dark night sky. This sinister creature dangles south, below the Zodiac band, curling his hook of a tail as if poised to attack with the menacing sting at its tip.

The centrepiece of his magnificent form is a flaming, ruby-coloured star. This supergiant is 300 times bigger than the Sun. We call it Antares, rival of the red planet Mars, but the Arabs knew it as 'the Heart of the Scorpion'.

The celestial Scorpion is truly ancient. For some 5000 years people have seen the shape of this fearsome creature in the pattern of the stars. To the people of Mesopotamia he was a symbol of might and darkness, sacred to the god of war.

When Scorpius rises in the eastern sky, the constellation Orion is sinking behind the horizon in the west. To the writers of ancient Greece, it seemed that the great Hunter's image in the sky was forever fleeing from the Scorpion, so they told how he had died from a scorpion's sting. So handsome and so skilled at hunting was the giant Orion, the legend ran, that the goddess Artemis allowed him to hunt with her. But Orion made a fatal mistake when he tried to embrace Artemis. Death by a scorpion's sting was his punishment for angering the vindictive goddess.

SAGITTARIUS

With muscles flexed and bow-string taut, the Archer aims straight for the heart of the Scorpion, his Zodiac neighbour. As a Centaur – part man, part horse – he stands perpetually poised to fire. But his arrow will never fly over the rich star-fields of the Milky Way that glitter between him and Scorpius. A massive black hole at the very centre of our Galaxy lies buried within these myriads of stars.

To the ancient people of Mesopotamia, the Archer was Pabilsag, a two-headed war-god. Son of the great god Enlil, this deity was a strange mixture of creatures. His body, like a Centaur's, was half-human, half-horse. Wings sprouted from his sides and on his shoulders sat the heads of both a man and a panther. His two tails were those of a horse and a scorpion. In his hands he carried a bow and arrow.

In the imagination of ancient Greek storytellers the Archer lost his wings, his panther-head and his scorpion's tail. Some said he was half-horse and half-man, though some pictured him as a satyr, like Pan. But he could not be a true Centaur for, according to Greek myths, no Centaur ever used a bow and arrow. So they invented a special tale about him. He was Crotus, whose mother was nurse to the Muses. The Muses so admired Crotus' musical talent and hunting skill, they asked Zeus to place him in the stars. Zeus represented him as an Archer-Centaur, to celebrate his hunting and riding prowess.

Capricornus

 With elegant horns and a long fish's tail, Capricornus is the fantastical Goat-Fish. This mythical beast is a symbol of great antiquity, more than 3000 years old. He stands for Ea, potent god of the Mesopotamians, who brought fresh water to the land.

No bright stars adorn Capricornus, the smallest Zodiac constellation. Algedi, lying at his head, seems to be the most luminous, but is actually two stars. Although they appear close to each other in the sky, in reality they are separated by trillions of miles of space.

Though dim, Capricornus was important to the people who worshipped Ea. In their time, three millennia ago, the yearly path of the Sun reached its farthest point south in the constellation Capricornus. This place in the sky was called the Gate of the Gods, where human souls ascended to heaven through the stars.

To explain a Goat-Fish in the Zodiac, ancient Greek writers told an ingenious story about the shepherd god, Pan. In a struggle for power between young gods and old, Zeus led the new gods of Olympus to victory over the Titans. To avenge the Titans' defeat, their mother Gaia sent a frightful monster called Typhoeus to attack Olympus. All the gods but Zeus fled to Egypt and turned themselves into animals. Pan, half-goat and half-man, dived into a river and was transformed into the Goat-Fish. Returning to land, Pan let out a shriek so awful that he frightened away Typhoeus, and grateful Zeus set the image of the Goat-Fish in the sky.

AQUARIUS

 Faint stars twinkle like sunlight glistening on a fountain where water cascades ceaselessly from Aquarius' jar. His form is outlined only by modest stars, the brightest two at his shoulders, but for 4000 years people have seen this constellation as a figure pouring liquid, or as an overflowing urn.

In ancient Mesopotamia he was the god Ea, the Great One, whose name means 'the House of Water'. He was the fount of knowledge and wisdom, but most of all the well-spring of fresh, life-giving water. In pictures of him, streams run from his shoulders or gush from urns grasped in his arms. In ancient Egypt, this constellation was a symbol of the River Nile, whose god, Hapi, poured water towards the heavens and the Earth.

Greek story-tellers said that the figure was Ganymede, cup-bearer to the gods, and some believed that the liquid spilling from his jar was not water, but nectar. The myth recounts that Ganymede was the most handsome of mortal youths and Zeus sent an eagle to carry him off from his father's home to serve the gods on Mount Olympus. There he became immortal, and Zeus changed both the Eagle and Ganymede into constellations.

PISCES

 Surely these slithery fishes could easily slip the cord that binds their tails! Yet, following a tradition more than 2000 years old, they are always joined by a shimmering ribbon of softly-glowing stars. One fish darts west towards the stream of water spilling from Aquarius' jar, while the other leaps north, as if to gulp the air. Though caught by their bond, Pisces can easily evade a sky-watcher's eye. The constellation's huge V-shape with a circlet at one tip is distinctive, but faint – only discernible on a truly dark night.

Who first pictured these stars as two fishes is a mystery. In Mesopotamia, some stars were seen as part of a swallow and some as part of a goddess. Others were called 'the Tails', but whether they were seen as fish-tails or the tail-feathers of a swallow, we cannot tell.

A story from ancient Greece says that Pisces represents Eros and Aphrodite, the god and goddess of love. One day they were by the River Euphrates when the towering monster Typhon appeared and threatened them. He was taller than a mountain, with snakes for legs. Fifty serpents hung from his hands in place of fingers, and fire blazed from his eyes. Terrified, Aphrodite and Eros leaped into the river and changed into fishes. They tied themselves together so as not lose each other as they swam to safety.

More about the Zodiac

The Sun's path

We cannot see the constellations during daylight because the sky is much too bright. If we could see them, we would notice that the Sun seems to move through the patterns of stars. We have the impression that Earth is standing still while the Sun travels around us, making a circuit of the sky once a year. In reality, Earth is orbiting the Sun and the stars are in the background, very much farther away than the Sun.

The Sun's path around the sky is called the ecliptic and it marks the centre of the Zodiac. Because Earth's equator is tilted at an angle of 23½° to its orbit, the ecliptic is tilted to the celestial equator by the same amount.

All the planets apart from Pluto revolve around the Sun close to one plane. As a result, their paths in the sky are never far from the ecliptic and pass through the Zodiac. The Moon's path is more complex but remains in or near the Zodiac band.

Constellations

Originally, people thought of constellations as patterns of bright stars. Later, they built on the idea to include areas of sky around the main formations. As more and more stars were discovered, astronomers were often confused about which constellations faint stars belonged to. So, in 1930, they agreed to split the whole sky into 88 constellation areas. The sizes of the constellations cover a huge range. Those in the Zodiac are all quite big but Virgo, the largest, has three times the area of the smallest, Capricornus.

The ecliptic goes through the twelve traditional constellations of the Zodiac but, because of the way the sky is now divided, it also goes through an extra one – Ophiuchus, the Serpent-Holder. And because the constellations are different sizes, the number of days it takes the Sun to move through them varies.

Signs

Astrologers divide the Zodiac belt into twelve equal sections called 'signs'. The idea was invented by the Babylonians in about 500 BC, as a convenient way of describing where the Sun, Moon and planets are. The signs have the same Latin names as the twelve traditional Zodiac constellations, except that astrologers say 'Capricorn' and 'Scorpio' instead of Capricornus and Scorpius. A person's astrological

Top left: Earth is tilted so its equator makes an angle of 23 ½° with its orbit around the Sun.
Centre: Viewed from Earth, the Sun moves around the sky along the ecliptic, which marks the centre of the Zodiac band. The ecliptic is tilted to the celestial equator by 23 ½°.

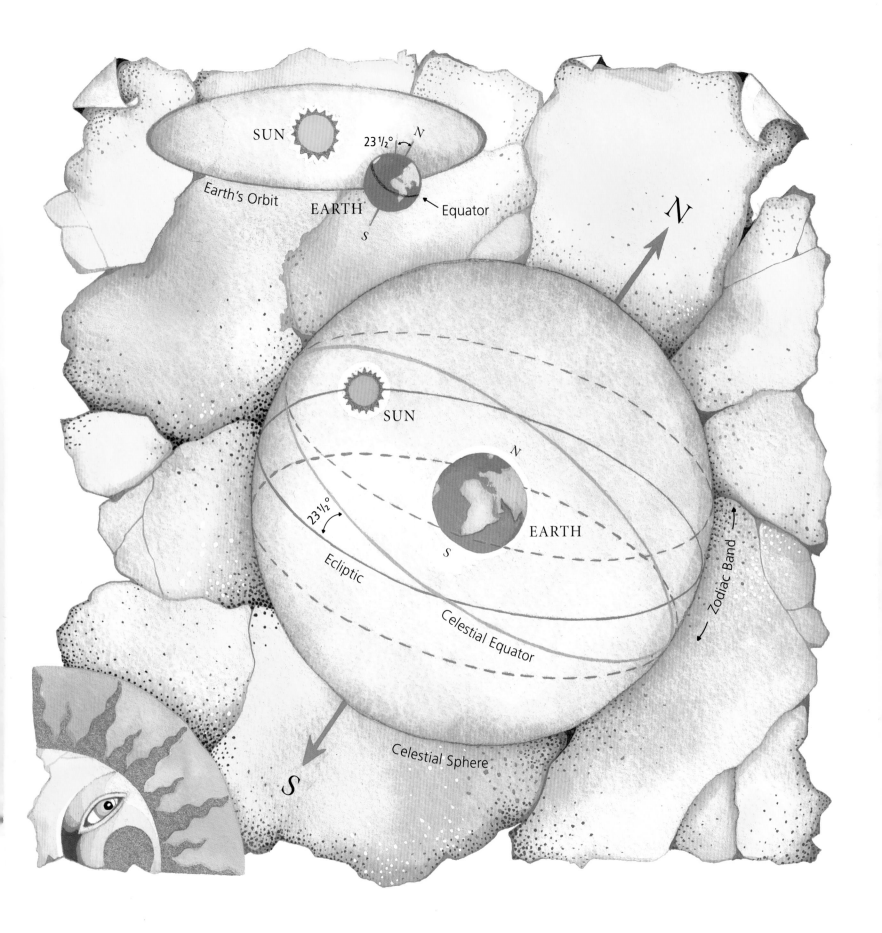

SUN

23½° N

Earth's Orbit

EARTH

Equator

S

N

SUN

23½°

N

S

EARTH

Ecliptic

Zodiac Band

Celestial Equator

Celestial Sphere

S

Zodiac sign is the one the Sun was in at the time of his or her birth.

When Zodiac astrology began about 2500 years ago, the signs coincided in the sky with the constellation patterns of the same name but, over the centuries, the signs and constellations have drifted apart due to a phenomenon astronomers call 'precession'. The stars remain in the same place but the reference point from which astrologers take the first of the signs, Aries, moves round the sky very slowly. That point is where the Sun crosses the celestial equator from south to north, an event that happens on the equinox in March. It is known as the First Point of Aries. Because Earth's axis 'wobbles' very slowly in space, the First Point of Aries slides along the ecliptic taking just over 2000 years to move from one sign to the next. At the moment, it is in the astronomical constellation Pisces.

The origin of the Zodiac

The word 'Zodiac' is derived from Greek and means 'circle of figures' or 'circle of living things'. But the Greeks did not invent the Zodiac. In about 500 BC they adopted a tradition that had its beginnings with the Sumerian civilisation in Mesopotamia in about 3200 BC. The concept of the Zodiac developed in stages up to the 6th century BC. The earliest known representations of the complete Zodiac are on clay tablets made several hundred years BC. When the Greeks adopted the Zodiac, their writers and poets began to link some of its figures with characters from their own mythology. But there was no general agreement on these associations and they were introduced long after the Zodiac had evolved into the form we know today.

The oldest constellations are Taurus, Leo, Scorpius and Aquarius. The Bull, the Lion and

the Scorpion were symbols of strength and power to the ancient Mesopotamians.

The Water Pourer (Aquarius) was Ea, god of life-giving fresh water, who was shown with streams of water running from each of his shoulders or hands. Ea was also represented as a goat with a fish's tail, the symbol that became Capricornus.

Though the Babylonians had a constellation called 'the Scales' (Libra). it was also known as 'the Claws of the Scorpion' by the Greeks. The matter was settled in favour of Libra by Julius Caesar, who represented himself on coins holding the scales of justice.

Gemini gets its name from two very bright stars, long known simply as 'the Twins'. We now call them Castor and Pollux.

The name 'Ear of Wheat' for Spica, the brightest star in Virgo, dates back to the Babylonians. At some stage, the dimmer stars around Spica began to be seen as the figure of a woman carrying the spike of corn.

Sagittarius, pictured as a centaur with a bow and arrow, originally may have been a Sumerian hunting god, Pabilsag. A centaur with a bow and arrow features in Babylonian art from 1000 BC or earlier, though the first Greek representations showed the Archer as a satyr rather than a centaur.

The origins of the faint constellations Pisces, Aries and Cancer remain even more mysterious. Historians may never discover for certain how they got their names.

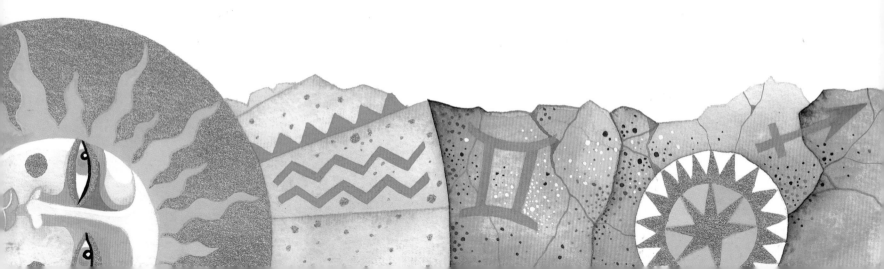

Astronomical constellations compared with astrological signs

The astrological signs of the Zodiac and the Zodiacal constellations used by astronomers occupy different areas on the sky even though they have the same names. This table shows the average dates when the Sun is in the sign and when it is in the constellation. In practice, the Sun does not move from one sign or constellation to the next at midnight, and actual dates in a particular year may be a day earlier or later than those given in the table. This variation happens because of the difference between the 365 ¼ days it takes Earth to travel round the Sun and the length of the calendar year, which may be 365 or 366 whole days.

Dates Sun is in traditional astrological sign	Name of constellation or sign	Dates Sun is in astronomical constellation
21 March – 19 April	ARIES	19 April – 13 May
20 April – 20 May	TAURUS	14 May – 19 June
21 May – 20 June	GEMINI	20 June – 20 July
21 June – 22 July	CANCER	21 July – 9 August
23 July – 22 August	LEO	10 August – 15 September
23 August – 22 September	VIRGO	16 September – 30 October
23 September – 22 October	LIBRA	31 October – 22 November
23 October – 21 November	SCORPIUS/SCORPIO	23 – 29 November
	OPHIUCHUS	30 November – 17 December
22 November – 21 December	SAGITTARIUS	18 December – 18 January
22 December – 19 January	CAPRICORN(US)	19 January – 15 February
20 January – 18 February	AQUARIUS	16 February – 11 March
19 February – 20 March	PISCES	12 March – 18 April

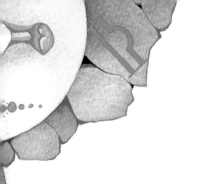

Visibility of Zodiac constellations in the sky

This table gives the dates on which the Zodiac constellations reach their highest point in the sky at midnight. From many locations they can be seen some time during the night for up to 3 months before or after these dates, but their visibility varies according to the observer's latitude and the position of the constellation in the sky in relation to the celestial equator.

Name of constellation	When highest in sky at midnight
Aries	30 October
Taurus	30 November
Gemini	5 January
Cancer	30 January
Leo	1 March
Virgo	11 April
Libra	9 May
Scorpius	3 June
Sagittarius	7 July
Capricornus	8 August
Aquarius	25 August
Pisces	27 September

7/14 ①